simple.

transparent.

uncluttered.

simple.

transparent.

uncluttered.

3 Strategies for Impactful Leadership

Kathleen Winter

Copyright ©2017 Kathleen Winter

All rights reserved
Published in the United States by CreateSpace

ISBN-13: 9781545277089

ISBN-10: 1545277087

Also by Kathleen Winter

New Leader Primer

Contents

	Introduction vii
One	simple. 1
	optimize outcomes 1
Two	transparent. 13
	we all know what we all know 13
Three	uncluttered. 28
	keeping what matters most the priority 28
Four	optimize 40
	lead with your strengths 40
	Reading List 49
	About the Author 51

Introduction

I've always wanted to simplify the complexities in my life. The complexities of where to live, how to spend my time, the professional relationships to develop or the corporate culture I found myself working in. Whether those complexities were self-inflicted or arose from life's circumstances, the busyness, drama, and unnecessary activities that they brought seemed to require extra energy from me but offer no payback or reward. I wanted simplicity.

I'm smart, educated, possess a somewhat high level of emotional intelligence (though we can all improve in that arena), and can handle complexity, but why do it? In the corporate environments I've been in over the past twenty-five years, I saw complexity rewarded many times when simple solutions, transparent communication, and uncluttered outcomes would have been optimal for customers, shareholders, and employees.

Why do I think this happened? At a fundamental level, complexity can drive exclusion—the exclusion of those who would contribute insight, perspective, and diverse points of view in strategy discussions and development processes for the target market. This is the exclusion of those who did not "fit"—those who did not go to the preferred school or look like the rest of the team.

I was guilty of exclusion and am writing this book to think through my decisions and their impact on others. I want to help you ask what the possibilities are for you to expand your life and your influence. If you are a leader at home, in your community, in your family, or if you run a business, the impact you can make with *simple.transparent.uncluttered.* strategies can be life changing.

simple.transparent.uncluttered.

In reflecting on my professional career, I can identify that it was the "exclusion culture" that chipped away at my core value of inclusiveness. The day I left the day-to-day corporate environment to simplify my life, becoming more transparent in my work coaching new leaders and helping businesses optimize their outcomes by staying true to my core values, my perspective shifted; for me, creating my professional work world was the right thing to do.

I hope that as you read this book, you will gain insight into your own core values and think about how *simple.transparent.uncluttered.* strategies can support you in optimizing both your impact as a leader and the impact of the teams you lead.

One

simple.
optimize outcomes

The image of a pair of untied tennis shoes on a teeter, as shown on the previous page, is one of my favorite pictures and always brings a smile to my face. The photo reminds me every day that life and leadership is a balancing challenge, but when executed with simplicity, this challenge can have great outcomes. Also refreshing in this photo is the vulnerability of the *simple* untied shoes. So many times we complicate analysis when a *simple* approach will get the best result. *Simple* can be the answer to inclusion. The great outcome of inclusiveness is diversity, and diversity can produce phenomenal results.

So how do simplicity and inclusion work? During my career in corporate America, as a finance director in a Fortune 50 company, I saw that operational leaders who managed the output of 90 percent of the workforce were expected to improve productivity, reduce costs, and exceed customer expectations. Every morning an operations conference call was held. All the many manufacturing and distribution locations reported on production and shipment results for the prior day, expected shipments for the current day, and any key obstacles. Each location was well prepared and could tell their operational story simply and effectively.

However, when the weekly cost meeting was held and financial questions were asked of the operations team (such as, "Why did overtime spending exceed the budget?"), there were blank stares from the operations team. These team members were the people who led those who made production happen; they were not accountants. The challenge in the cost meeting was how the questions were framed by the finance team. The finance team was using accounting language instead of operational language.

One of the first things I did was encourage the finance analysts to sit in on the daily operations call to help accelerate their learning of operations and convert the language used in the cost meetings to operational language. The analysts were welcomed into the operations meetings, and soon the cost meetings were a *simple* collaboration about the business, with all in the room understanding the questions and the goals. By expanding the analysts' views by including them in the operations call, and thus helping both the finance and operations teams learn new languages, the bond between the two teams grew, and the cost-review meetings became more forward looking on how to change the company's trajectory (instead of primarily looking back). It was a win-win situation for all.

I have been a successful finance partner to operations teams for most of my career. I respected their drive, sincerity, customer focus, and in most cases, their leadership. I knew from experience that when the financial story was told about their decisions, they had ownership, but only if they could tell the story themselves. My finance teams and I transformed the cost deck into one that the operations leaders could share with their teams and so improve the financial acumen by connecting actions to financial results. The executives in operations and finance also came to rely on this *simple* version.

By working in small, cross-functional teams to create this deck, *the* story became *our* story. Teams then understood that in some cases, exceeding shipment targets didn't necessarily mean achieving revenue targets. They understood that product mix and sometimes overtime costs versus new-hire costs were more favorable to the bottom line. You see, the operational teams could have the greatest impact on bottom-line outcomes through their decision making.

By simplifying the story, sharing basic knowledge, and connecting the two worlds of finance and operations, the operations team could better understand the outcomes of its decisions and was able to make operational calls that were based on knowledge and understanding.

Think about how you can *simplify* your message for the greatest impact.

I once supported a general manager who said, "The shareholders give us one dollar and expect one dollar twenty-five cents back." That is what leadership in business does. Shareholders trust us with their money, and because we are the leaders and managers of processes, we are expected to provide a return. This manager was very effective at understanding the operations teams and communicating with them for optimal results. He shared his vision in a simple manner that connected with his team. He was also committed to developing well-rounded leaders in the organization and was a true believer in diversity and inclusion. During my tenure with the company, I sometimes did not appreciate his style, but I certainly learned from and respected him.

Peers and leaders said "keep it simple" many times throughout my career. I'm sure you have heard this said and perhaps have even said it yourself a few times.

I believe in the saying, but it is the *spirit* behind the delivery that causes me to pause when I hear it. You see, in some cases the statement is made out of disrespect; in other cases it is made to promote inclusiveness. So ask yourself, how do you use this statement? Be real with your answer. You are not required to post your answer on Twitter, Facebook or

LinkedIn. An honest answer to yourself will help you to become the leader your team deserves.

Let's say the statement was made out of disrespect. The assumption is that the receivers of the message are less educated, less experienced, and not as capable or as "IQ smart" as the speaker (we will discuss EQ, emotional-intelligence quotient, later). If you use this statement in this way, I'd encourage you to keep reading this book for a different perspective.

However, if you use this statement to promote inclusion, then read this book intently to find insights and strategies to help you use *simple.transparent.uncluttered.* to optimize outcomes for you and your team.

Organizations don't have cloned talent pools, with everyone at the same IQ, experience level, or education level. If you harbor value judgments about technical skills versus knowledge skills, then try calling a coder when you need a plumber or asking an accountant to repair your car.

Engines these days require exceptional technical talent, and you require a car that operates, so telling your accountant the check-engine light comes on or that your car is exhausting black smoke doesn't improve the outcome. If your business is focused on improving outcomes in a car service center, accountants, automotive technicians, service writers, and facilities people all need to work together and understand the mission of the business.

You are the leader and are responsible for optimizing outcomes. If your leadership message and behavior exclude those who actually do the work or interface with the customer you and your company will fail.

One key element to leveling the playing field in your organization is EQ (emotional-intelligence quotient). Dr. Travis Bradberry explains EQ in *Emotional Intelligence 2.0*. He and his coauthor Jean Greaves write a simple approach for how you, as an individual, can improve your outcomes by understanding your reactions to your own and others' emotions and managing those emotions for an optimized outcome.

simple.transparent.uncluttered.

Bradberry and Greaves provide simple, actionable tasks that will improve your self-management and increase the likelihood of positive outcomes in relationship management.

Think about the car service center scenario. Imagine an automotive service center where accountants, technicians, service writers, and facilities team members all understand cost, productivity, customer service, and their individual roles in ensuring the customer is served. The facilities person could be your next service writer, your accountant could manage an expansion, and your technicians could lead new-hire classes. When cross-functional problem solving occurs, a "common communication culture" drives results, and the profit line improves. Through a culture of *simple*, you provide a vision for inclusion and create teams that thrive on winning!

The "continuous improvement" and "lean" philosophies used in the corporate space foundationally require inclusion. The goal of being lean is to eliminate waste in a process. Through process mapping of the current state, waste is identified and eliminated with a future-state map created. This future state should reflect the process used to create a product that the customer is willing to purchase. The process-mapping dynamic requires input from all those involved in the process chain—they need to participate, understand, and be heard.

One of my most treasured awards is the "Simplify and Go" award I received while working at Nike. During that time, finance teams were taking half a month to close the financial systems and report results with commentary. Data reported too long after the event can be useless if course correction is needed. Even with integrated systems, the process was longer than needed, and the new goal was to report results within two business days.

A schedule compression can cause unnecessary tension, inaccurate commentary, and overall anxiety if not presented holistically. I've experienced poor rollouts of schedule compression, and finance teams bear the unnecessary pain while internal business partners rebel against accelerated deadlines.

simple.transparent.uncluttered.

We decided at the Nike distribution centers to include our internal customers (DC managers) in our planning session on how to improve processes to meet the new reporting goal. The two teams worked well together, each putting their skin in the game, and they eliminated the waste in the process. I was so proud of the cross-functional team. They also received much-earned awards, and by the time I moved companies, the DC managers' financial acumen was substantially improved, and the finance team better understood product flow, people management, and productivity.

The value of *simple* drives inclusion and produces outstanding results!

STRATEGIES TO *SIMPLE*

- Rotate ownership of the KPI (key performance indicators) among the team members.
- Annual assessment of each KPI for relevancy.
- Have a new team member review your last formal communication and ask questions on the topics that are unclear to them.
- Encourage cross-functional shadow assignments.
- Reduce the number of your last project presentation pages by half and then in half again, and keep the complete message.

Two

transparent.
we all know what we all know

Transparency is a multifaceted topic and worth defining at the outset. According to The Business Dictionary the business definition of "transparency" is:

The lack of hidden agendas or conditions, accompanied by the availability of full information required for collaboration, cooperation, and collective decision making.

The transparency we practice in managing our professional, social, and personal lives varies in degrees. Although some would challenge that with social media, we have all signed up for transparency, I don't subscribe to that perspective, and here is why.

In our personal and social lives, we participate at the level we choose when sharing our activities, concerns, challenges, and passions with others. The details of our feelings, the fears we are experiencing, and how we overcame those fears are usually shared with whom we choose. The only guidelines or boundaries are the ones we create ourselves.

simple.transparent.uncluttered.

How many times have you "liked" an article on Facebook because you wanted to be part of the group? You didn't have sufficient information on the topic, your instincts caused you to pause, but you wanted to be part of the group. You chose to parse your belief, shared only a portion of your thought, and moved on.

Partial transparency can be a strategy in our personal and social lives. You will pick and choose just as others pick and choose, so when you ask others in your personal or social life to be transparent, hold yourself to the same standard.

However, being transparent as a leader, manager, or supervisor in a corporation calls upon us to manage our individual core values alongside the core values of the company as well as with ethics and laws. When there is a gap between your core values and those of the company you are a part of, the internal conflict can be difficult to manage.

What if transparency had been a core value of the General Motors engineering group and its executives?

How many lives would have been saved when calling out a faulty ignition system? What if British Petroleum's offshore workers on the *Deepwater Horizon* had worked in a culture that required safety at all costs and insisted on transparency in reporting safety violations? What if transparency was a core value at Countrywide Financial and mortgages had not been given to people who couldn't pay them back? What if the senior executives at Wells Fargo focused on ethical strategies to drive growth and took ethics hotline complaints as serious indictments of a culture driven by unrealistic goals?

In the instances above, millions of shareholders investments were paid out in claims, innocent employees' lives have been impacted, and the customer's trust was eroded. There is a saying that just because it is legal, doesn't mean it is ethical. Be prepared to ask yourself where is your line and what will you do if you are expected to cross it?

The good news is that the financial and personal rewards in being a responsible, *transparent* leader

simple.transparent.uncluttered.

can generate extraordinary outcomes. There were news articles written about challenges large and small businesses were having during the 2008 recession that told heartwarming stories of companies and coworkers working together to mitigate the impacts during that time.

During the 2008 recession, businesses that were transparent with their employees about the state of the business and the changes needed to keep people working saw individuals come forward willing to take greater cuts from their share, knowing others needed the income more. When coworkers had serious illnesses and had exhausted their sick time, workers would donate their accumulated hours. When manufacturing companies would shift work overseas to support a growing market, the workers continued their high level of quality and productivity through the last day.

I've seen from my own experience that when there was a food drive, coat drive, or fund raiser for Juvenile Diabetes Research Foundation, those who could least afford it always came to the plant with their arms full of donations. They did this because their core values of giving to others, along with the high level of trust for the leaders of the locations, created this culture.

In leadership, "transparency" means:

- Share what you can.
- If you know and can't share, then say so.
- If you don't know, then say you don't know.

All three strategies have to be communicated with sincerity and honesty. We know when others are spinning the story, and we feel offended and distrustful. Don't offend your team, colleagues, or executives by not being transparent. If you are in an organization that rewards dishonest spin and secrecy, ask yourself if those are your values. My grandmother always reminded me that birds of a feather flock together.

Check yourself!

Our challenge with transparent communication can sometimes be in living out the strategy that if you

simple.transparent.uncluttered.

know and can't share, then you should say so. In several of the companies I worked for, I was in finance roles. These roles are usually the ones that prepare business cases to open and close locations and discontinue products or services, and each scenario can significantly impact the people you work with and work for.

In one of my roles, I had a front-row seat to witness the impact that lack of transparency has on organizations. I was assigned to create a business case for outsourcing manufacturing and distribution and the subsequent location closures for a Fortune 100 company. Midway through the business-case development, after the decision was made to execute the outsourcing strategy, senior executives made a visit to a manufacturing plant and presented an optimistic outlook to the workforce in an all-hands meeting.

That lack of transparency by the senior executives challenged my values. The challenge to my values was not because of the strategic business case but the deception perpetuated by the executives against the workforce. There were ways to tell the story about shifting markets, but they took the easy and least honest way out. In addition the politics that determined who was in the know were outrageous, underhanded, and certainly not the best the company had to offer.

Over the next ten months, I saw the manipulation of the production allocations to favor one location over the other, and I saw costs being reported that were inaccurate, all because people were protecting "their" location. Instead of preparing to outsource, the infighting continued.

So-called leaders were protecting their organizations at the expense of others, adding additional complexity to processes that were not necessary in order to drive failure in the new provider, and they were not transparent about the progress of the transition. In my opinion, this behavior was all about self-protection. The effort spent trying to sabotage others would have been better spent preparing the workforce (executives, engineers, and assemblers) to exit

simple.transparent.uncluttered.

the business with the skills and experience to continue their lives.

So what would a *transparent* strategy look like in this case? In the all-hands meeting, I would have shared information about the global shift in the market and the business strategy to adjust as well as high-level time lines. I would have given a broad timeline, given incremental performance pay (think about cost of the golden parachutes enjoyed by senior executives!), begun retraining efforts, and earned the pay I received as a leader by being present, accountable, and *transparent* until the doors closed.

I know many examples where this occurred, but I know even more examples of when the sixty-day notice was served up and no leadership figures helped to prepare the employees for their next phase. I've always considered former employees to be future customers of the business, especially if the business is consumer driven.

In this particular case, I broke confidence and shared the information with an operations manager after he was lied to by his senior executive in front of me, the same executive who had assigned me to work on the business case. I had supported this operations director and knew he would and could impact how this eventual closure impacted his team. I got called out on this by an even more senior executive, but there were no repercussions, and I was still trusted with plum assignments.

Sometimes we just have to vote according to our conscience.

In manufacturing, distribution, or even laboratories, the people who do the work know when the hum of the factory, distribution center, or lab is low; when inbound materials, products, or specimens are slow; when customer orders or patient medical results become fewer; and when working hours are reduced. Knowledge workers know when the project lists begin to get shorter, when they are being asked to cross-train or document work processes, and when the financial results continue to fade.

simple.transparent.uncluttered.

So, as a leader, don't sell your teams short, and *share what you can.*

Leadership positions require discretion and confidentiality as a character trait. The information that leaders sometimes are required to keep confidential can have a great impact on others, with an added responsibility of being truthful. I've been a key participant on acquisition teams that are responsible for, at times, not only due diligence in purchasing another company in order to expand market share, eliminate competition, or gain access to a certain technology but that led integration teams after the purchase.

The financial story always includes *synergies*—meaning eliminating duplication in processes (people), reallocating services and production strategies, and above all, keeping the transition seamless for customers. Post acquisition and post integration kick-off always has the opening line "welcome to the family," while the integration plan lays out the synergy implementations. While the acquiring company executives look to expand their sphere of influence and protect their current team, I've seen the purchased company employees listen politely to inclusionary messages while watching their coworkers being eliminated for duplication. There was very little attention paid to creating a new culture that took the best from both companies. Although the formal communications always included a best-of-both-companies approach, the actions taken were inconsistent.

The fundamental value of transparency is being truthful about the plan. The buying company may not be transparent with the purchased company at all. I struggled leading these integrations. I knew the purchase strategy well, I understood the potential financial benefits of best-of-both approach, but I became increasingly skeptical as I watched my peers let great people exit—people who, only a year earlier, were kicking our behinds in the marketplace. I truly kept the best of both groups in *my* group, but I was the only one who did. No surprise, a year after the purchase, the financial synergies had not happened, customers fled the new organization, and a big acquisition cost turned into a financial write-off.

Acquisitions can be difficult, but business is difficult. Being a responsible, transparent leader not only keeps your current team aware of the strategy and how they might be a part of the new organization but provides a forum for the new team to show their best. Being a responsible, transparent leader means sharing openly the value of the acquisition and what the new company can become, with employees' efforts and talent. We all want to know the answer to the question, Where and how do I fit in this new company?

Be a transparent leader, and help each employee create his or her own success!

During my research for this book, there were many articles I read on the need for transparency in business, so I will give credit where credit is due. One article in particular, written by Sam Hodges, the cofounder and US managing director of Funding Circle, published on August 21, 2016, in *Entrepreneur*, focused on four ways to be transparent. Hodges wrote:

- *Promote candid conversations with your team*
- *Access to information isn't enough, provide context, commentary and clarity*
- *Teach people how to give and receive honest feedback*
- *Proactively share bad news*

The big challenge here is being upfront, honest and reassuring without provoking alarm, unrest or distraction from broader team goals. Use your discretion on the best channel to deliver the news, and then work with a small team you trust to nail your narrative and key messages around the perceived problem and your game plan. In my experience, teams that openly embrace mistakes as learning opportunities are less likely to be disrupted by big shifts or bad news in the long run.

simple.transparent.uncluttered.

STRATEGIES TO *TRANSPARENT*

- Be responsibly transparent in actions and words.
    - If you don't know, then say you don't know.
    - If you know and can't share, say so.
    - Share what you can.
- When we know how we fit in an organization, we do better.
- Continue improving your emotional intelligence through recognizing the emotions of others and managing your reactions to those emotions.

Three

uncluttered.
keeping what matters most the priority

simple.transparent.uncluttered.

Have you ever been in an executive's or a peer's workspace or office to have a conversation about a specific project or strategy and seen piles of papers covering the work surface and floor and piles of books everywhere? Did you find yourself distracted by the piles of stuff, or did your colleague seem distracted and focused on his or her piles and not on the conversation? Did he or she search the piles for a piece of paper or book to share that supported your conversation? Did you leave the conversation feeling somewhat frustrated, distracted, and disrespected or feeling engaged, informed, and focused?

I've encountered a few peers and executives who had workspaces that looked like a tornado just passed through them. I admit, I'm the kind of person with a clean desktop—there are a couple of folders on top of my work surface, but I keep my project files out of sight until I work on them. My electronic files are also organized and only in play when I am working on them.

I always dreaded meetings in cluttered spaces. We always seemed to end those meetings with fewer decisions made and more follow-ups needed. Time was spent looking for a piece of paper or a book that might support the argument. Sharing a hardcopy of a project plan always meant I brought extra because the other person never was able to find theirs. Even when using electronic methods, he or she seemed unable to find the relevant folder or document on shared drives. Their electronic desk looked like their real desk: cluttered and without priority.

What about having an online meeting where the slides or visuals don't support the topic or there are many slides or visuals that are seemingly wordy and unclear? How do you feel after the meeting has ended? Are you able to recap the story in a few simple sentences to share with others, without feeling like you have to sort through the BS?

Have you been in a simple phone conversation where you can hear paper rustling, external noise,

simple.transparent.uncluttered.

and frequent phone mutes? How do you feel when you end what you had considered an important conversation?

These are all very real examples of our experiences in the corporate world today. Communications are not always face-to-face and in an orderly conference room where the physical environment is not a hindrance to the process. Our communication channels are varied, and if we aren't mindful of keeping an *uncluttered* approach, then the outcome is the same as meeting face-to-face in the office full of piles!

So, how can you create an *uncluttered* approach in your communications? The three areas I focus on are:

- Creating a space and delivery method that is most impactful to the audience (the how)
- Understanding your audience and their need to know (the who)
- Communicating with simple clarity (the what)

Creating a space and delivery method that supports your team isn't that challenging. It is a matter of making sure the logistics of the meetings are fundamental by adopting a few simple rules of engagement.

- Mute phones to eliminate distractions.
- Speak clearly and at a volume all can hear.
- Avoid side conversations.
- Make sure the technology works.
- Ensure all participants can see the same presentation.

I have a lot of experience working in a non corporate location and being on the receiving end of conference calls. Although I could discount a less-than-stellar phone connection, the side conversations for me were a sign of disrespect, and not being sent the same materials being viewed by the majority of the team in the room added to the feeling of disconnection. These are serious communication failures that are easily overcome in order to *unclutter* your communication approach.

simple.transparent.uncluttered.

Understanding your audience and their need to know will guide you in uncluttering the communication materials. I made the mistake, early in my career, of preparing and presenting financial results to financial peers and operations teams by using the same material. The discussions in the finance-team reviews would focus on Generally Accepted Accounting Principles (GAAP)and corporate allocations, while operational performance was a footnote. The operations teams wanted to know how their decisions impacted financial results and were not so interested in the GAAP or corporate allocations that were booked below the earnings before interest and taxes (EBIT) line. So, after several sessions, I finally got it; I changed up the operations deck and focused on the financial outcomes the operations team could impact. I have to tell you, I was proud of every operations team I supported as they learned and understood and then made decisions that improved financial outcomes.

So review the meeting's attendee list and ask yourself why those attending need to know this information.

Then take responsibility for creating a way to deliver the information for maximum impact.

Uncluttering a detailed message takes skill, knowledge, and an awareness of the audience. The language used in conversations with investors regarding improved or declining profits and strategy changes is different than that used in communications when employees are impacted. I'm not implying anything about intelligence; I'm challenging you to unclutter the story and deliver the communication so it is heard and understood.

The third area of focus, communicate with simple clarity, means: don't take fifteen minutes when five will do. Leave enough time for questions and additional discussion. The employee who willingly asks a question in a room of fifty or even ten means there are others in the room with the same question. This is a chance to keep what matters most as the priority in front of the audience.

I'm not a communications expert; however, I've seen what works in a multitude of environments (on

simple.transparent.uncluttered.

manufacturing floors, in distribution centers, finance teams, senior executive meetings, sales teams, and even in individual one-on-ones), and the common theme is: Why are you telling me this, and how does it impact me? So craft your message to answer these questions.

Why is being *uncluttered* important, and how can you get there? To be uncluttered is to keeping what matters most as the priority. We all have to-do lists, calendars that are overscheduled, and conflicting multiple priorities. In our culture, those perceived as busy people are viewed as more valuable, but when the curtain is pulled back, it most often reveals that what matters most isn't getting things done—the *busyness* is what got rewarded, not the results. I've used the phrase "don't confuse actions with results" many times in working with colleagues and teams that think having a full calendar or multiple priorities means they are getting results.

As a leader, identifying what matters *most* is one of the key principles.

How many times have you participated in a brainstorming or priority-setting session and the group comes up with ten "number one" priorities and only enough resources to accomplish five of the ten? Team dynamics and individual feelings of frustration about not being able to create and execute a great solution can impact morale and creativity and eventually can become detrimental to the culture.

In many corporate cultures that overcommit, the five priorities that are accomplished are overshadowed by the "failure" of the other five left undone. This approach is self-defeating and leads a corporate downward spiral that results in broken promises to customers, lower individual and group morale, and missed gains for shareholders.

Leaders are responsible for creating and living a culture that keeps what matters most as the priority. Engaged and competent leaders understand the importance of employee engagement in financially successful companies, and they keep what matters most the priority. Leaders create the vision, guide teams to strategies that are realistic, and support failure as a way to discovering the solutions. These leaders resist overcommitting and so not delivering. The leader who resists the pressure to overcommit can be politically challenging in most corporate environments, but executing plans and driving bottom-line results is rewarded.

For me, one of the most satisfying rewards is trust and integrity—trust from my team, colleagues, and senior executives that can culminate in greater opportunities for my team and myself. No one wants to be on a team that has no playbook, never wins, and always disappoints the fans. Be the coach of your team by committing to the game with integrity.

So, how do you build trust? Building trust literally starts the day you interview with the company, and it continues with every interaction thereafter. Your actions in keeping appointments on time; being respectful, courteous, engaged; and being a sponge (listening and observing) are all part of the foundation to building trust. To add to that list: treat others how you would want to be treated, listen more than you talk, and be available and approachable to all.

I share these actions based on lessons I've learned; throughout my career I've made plenty of mistakes in building trust. I was shortsighted by not listening enough (although I am an extreme introvert, I flipped my on switch a lot!), I struggled with being approachable (an issue I had as a woman in a leadership position before this was socially "acceptable"), and I was quick to exclude those whose opinions were far different from mine. I often took a flight-or-fight stance unnecessarily. I know I've learned through my mistakes, and when working with new clients, I make sure I become a sponge: I listen intently. And I use techniques that can bring diverse strategies and opinions to the table for discussion and resolution. I've also discovered that when sharing the end game with a new client, being a sponge and listening intently sets the tone and starts building trust.

Ask yourself: How can you improve your leadership impact by keeping *what matters most* as the priority?

simple.transparent.uncluttered.

STRATEGIES TO *UNCLUTTERED*

- Keep what matters most the priority.
- Communicate with an understanding of your audience.
- Be the leader who commits with trust and integrity.
- Reflect on your style and adjust course to become the great leader you can be.

Four

optimize
lead with your strengths

simple.transparent.uncluttered.

Throughout my career I frequently did a personal debrief after leaving one company and before starting another. I would create a list of my successes and failures, for my eyes only, and be brutally honest with myself, based on feedback I'd received during my time at the company and my personal assessment of my experience there.

The list was not about the professional accomplishments or promotions, opening/ or closing locations, or new skills I learned but about how I impacted and treated the people I worked with and for and the individuals on the teams I was responsible for. Over time, the list has become a reflection of my values and of how I live out those values in my actions with others. My experiences were rich in lessons learned.

I also solicited feedback from a couple of trusted people I have known over the course of my career. I never shared the details of this debrief with my confidants, but I asked questions about their perspective and observations and certainly took their feedback seriously.

This process not only supported my emotional transition but provided a process to evaluate my lessons learned, progress, and setbacks.

I wanted to keep my list *simple.transparent.uncluttered*. It contained three columns, which addressed the following questions:

- What went well?
- What didn't go well?
- What do I want to change in myself?

I discovered that my commitment to a level playing field and to transparency created internal conflict for me. I rarely struggled with *simple* and *uncluttered* but as mentioned earlier, *transparent* was and will always be a challenge in business and was one of my greatest sources of conflict.

simple.transparent.uncluttered.

These debriefs helped me to reaffirm my values, course correct, and over time, play to my strengths. I'd recommend this debrief process to anyone.

Take some quiet time, ask yourself the three questions above, and be honest with yourself in your answer. Seek trusted counsel as you develop your *simple.transparent.uncluttered.* leadership style.

There are many self-discovery, self-help, and leadership books and articles available to guide you on your path. I've read many of these books, and I have a few favorite authors (see the Reading List that follows), but there is no substitute for learning and understanding your internal voice. Learning who you are as a person is a continuous, lifelong process. Our interests, our approach to challenges, and the business environment we choose to engage in can change; our curiosity can take us down interesting paths, if we are willing to go.

When I reflect on my journey, I sometimes ask myself "What was I thinking?" with a chuckle, knowing and truly believing that when we know better, we do better.

Playing to your strengths is powerful. The earlier in your career you discover and nurture them, the more internal satisfaction you will have.

I wasn't so aware early in my career. I was good at simplifying complexity, getting to the bottom line, and executing to the goal, but I wasn't fully aware of how to be effective in using the *simple.transparent. uncluttered* strategy combination to be as effective and influential as possible. My performance reviews always gave me high ratings on change management, exceeding goals, and quantity of work, but there was almost no conversation about how to *optimize* the combination of my strengths and fold in the necessary component of managing relationships.

What do your performance reviews tell you about your strengths?

I'm so relieved to see the annual performance-review process being eliminated by progressive companies.

simple.transparent.uncluttered.

It was a source of anxiety for employees and also leaders. Each knew that surprise comments were a reflection of poor communication throughout the year, and although highlighting accomplishments is useful, the formal review process rarely addresses plans to play to strengths; rather, it focused on changing the weaknesses.

How will you change your conversations with your teams?

My corporate moves were primarily to explore different industries, different cultures, and different areas in the country. I've worked in finance and supply chain in heavy manufacturing, in high-end furniture design, specialty chemicals, distribution, technology, and biotech.

I've lived in Texas (Houston, Austin, and Dallas), Tennessee (Memphis and Nashville), and North Carolina (Charlotte). I grew up in Southern California, so the changes I experienced in living in all those locations presented changes in geography, politics, and culture. Even the subcultures of specific locations separate from the corporate headquarters were different. I worked for Nike in Memphis, Tennessee, and its headquarters are in Beaverton, Oregon. I worked for Dell in Nashville, Tennessee, and its headquarters are in Round Rock, Texas. I led a supply-chain organization with laboratories from Boston to the West Coast, with that company's headquarters in Dallas.

The multiple moves, the variation in industry and geography all were foundational to me becoming aware of my strengths and learning to *optimize* the impact of *simple.transparent.uncluttered.*

I can truthfully say I've always liked the challenge of living new places, except where there are large amounts of snow. As you can tell by the places I've lived, I'm a moderate-weather person!

I feel enriched by the corporate experiences I have had and continue to have in my consulting business. I have no regrets about the time I spent at the companies I worked with, the geographical moves I made, or the lessons I learned from my debriefs during my

simple.transparent.uncluttered.

formal career. I know my strengths as risk taker and as someone who is adaptable, curious, and results focused. I can read a room better now and be more mindful of others, and I choose to focus on issues that really matter to me and drive necessary change.

Who are you, and what are your strengths?

STRATEGIES TO *OPTIMIZE*

- Learn who you are.
- Lead with your strengths.
- Create a personal career debrief.

Reading List

Altucher, James. *Choose Yourself*. United States: Lioncrest Publishing, 2017

Bradberry, Travis., Greaves, Jean. *Emotional Intelligence 2.0*.United States: TalentSmart, 2009

Buckingham, Marcus. *Now, Discover Your Strengths*. New York, NY: The Free Press, 2001

Mastromonaco, Alyssa. *Who Thought This Was a Good Idea?*. New York, NY: Twelve Hatchett Book Group, 2017

Mohr, Tara. *Playing Big*. New York, NY: Gotham Books, 2014

Morall, Michael. *The Great War of Our Time*. New York, NY: Twelve Hatchett Book Group, 2015

Sinek, Simon. *Start With Why*. New York, NY: Penguin Group, 2009

About the Author

Kathleen Winter is the principal at Winter Consulting, her independent business-operations consulting practice. Her practice focuses on helping businesses optimize results using a *simple.transparent.uncluttered.* approach.

Kathleen worked for over two decades in corporate America, in finance and supply-chain roles. In this book she shares her leadership experiences from Nike, Dell, Thomas & Betts, Lucite, and Miraca Life Sciences, advocating a strategic leadership foundation that is *simple.transparent.uncluttered.*

Kathleen grew up in Southern California in an economically poor family. She is a proud product of the California public school system, with a BS in business from the University of Redlands. She started her business career in Houston, Texas, and has enjoyed living throughout the southern United States. While developing her career, Kathleen obtained an MBA from the University of Memphis.

Kathleen is currently living in the wine country of Southern California while she writes and works on business endeavors. She is interested in learning about your *simple.transparent.uncluttered.* journey.

Winter Consulting
PO Box 836
Aguanga, CA 92536
www.kathleenwinterconsulting.com
kathleen@kathleenwinterconsulting.com

www.ingramcontent.com/pod-product-compliance
Lightning Source LLC
Chambersburg PA
CBHW061446180526
45170CB00004B/1586